January Rides
the Wind

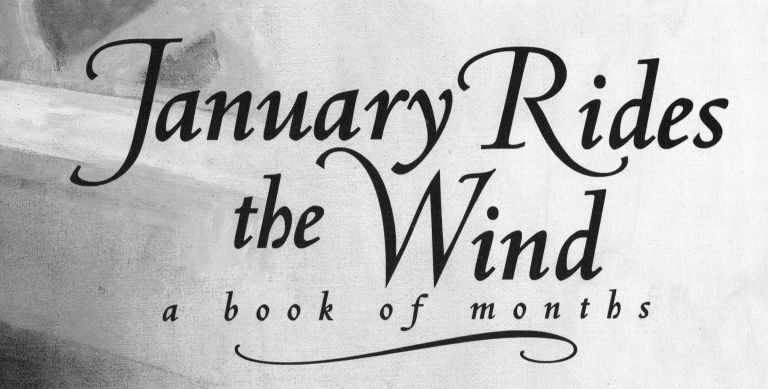

January Rides the Wind
a book of months

by Charlotte F. Otten
illustrated by Todd L. W. Doney

Lothrop, Lee & Shepard Books • Morrow

New York

For Bob

—C.O.

*To my boys' grandmother,
Beverly Doney*

—T.D.

Oil paints were used for the full-color illustrations. The text type is 18-point Goudy Old Style.

Text copyright © 1997 by Charlotte F. Otten
Illustrations copyright © 1997 by Todd L.W. Doney

Published by Lothrop, Lee & Shepard Books
an imprint of Morrow Junior Books
a division of William Morrow and Company, Inc.
1350 Avenue of the Americas, New York, NY 10019

Printed in the United States of America.

1 2 3 4 5 6 7 8 9 10

Library of Congress Cataloging-in-Publication Data
Otten, Charlotte F.
January rides the wind: a book of months / by Charlotte Otten; illustrated by Todd L.W. Doney.
p. cm.
Summary: Twelve poems, one describing each month.
ISBN 0-688-12556-5 (trade)—ISBN 0-688-12557-3 (library)
1. Months—Juvenile poetry.   2. Children's poetry, American.   [1. Months—Poetry.   2. American poetry.]
I. Doney, Todd, ill.   II. Title.   PS3565.T75J36 1997   811'.54—dc20   92-44159   CIP AC

January

January rides the wind,
sideswipes deer and rabbits.
Their white tails billow
like pillowcases on the line.

February

February turns everything to gray:
gray lakes, gray fog, gray sun.
Gray squirrels lose their bearings
hunting for acorns buried
beneath thick gray snow.

March

March eats the winter;
icicles drip from its mouth
to fall on secret gardens.
Crocuses wake,
stain the melting snow with gold.

April

April sings soft songs to willows,
calls newts to crawl from creeks.
Yesterday at four
a cardinal called his sweet mate
to the feeder.

May

May's arms are filled with babies,
she spills them everywhere.
Lambs stumble, foals fumble
for their mothers. Apple trees
drop blossoms on the earth.

June

June measures time
until the longest day
becomes the shortest night.
Fireflies ignite, pushing
dark aside.

July

July pumps dry heat into the ground.
Grasses sing, cicadas harp,
spiders stretch their lanky legs.
Dry thunder echoes
in a flash of light.

August

August sweats.
Blueberries, bilberries,
blackberries, sugar plums
burst into purple juice,
stain our fingers, tongues, and teeth.

September

September squeezes what is left of summer
into night-cool cider.
Squashes, pumpkins, red potatoes
huddle in Earth's basket.
Concord-grape skins split,
stabbed by sucking bees.

October

October smolders.
Leaves flare up in rivers.
Migrant geese honk
and break the morning sky.

November

November swaddles stars,
swims in polar light.
Red foxes dance on stones
lit by the moon.

December

December runs to darkness,
shortens days,
stretches night to night,
stockpiles badgers, bears, and bats…
holds its breath for spring.

About the Author

"When I was a child, Sunday evenings were special because of my father's storytelling," says Charlotte Otten. "It wasn't until years later that I realized he hadn't made up the stories of David Copperfield and Oliver Twist himself!"

Charlotte is a poet and the editor of *The Book of Birth Poetry*. This is her first children's book. She lives with her husband, Robert, in a house overlooking Plaster Creek in Grand Rapids, Michigan, where they like to watch the changing of the seasons. The Ottens have two grown sons and two grandchildren.

About the Artist

"A visual feast," said *Kirkus Reviews* of Todd Doney's illustrations for *Red Bird,* by Barbara Mitchell.

Todd grew up in Chicago, where he earned his degrees in fine art and illustration from the American Academy of Art. He is the illustrator of several books for children, including *Sleeping Beauty: The Ballet Story* (Atheneum) and *Old Salt, Young Salt,* by Jonathan London. Todd currently lives in Morristown, New Jersey. He is the father of two young sons, Reid and Jesse.

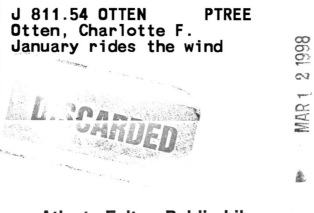